The Rai...

Written and photographed by Fred Fusselman
Illustrated by Ralph Whirly

An iguana

A butterfly

A monkey

A macaw

You can find the definitions of **boldfaced** words used in this book on pages 30 and 31.

Contents

What Is a Rain Forest?	4
Layers of the Rain Forest	6
The Forest Floor	8
The Understory	10
The Lower Canopy	12
The Upper Canopy	14
People of the Rain Forest	16
How the Ecosystem Works	18
Ecosystems in Danger	20
Destruction	22
Conservation	24
Preservation: Butterflies	26
From the Author/Photographer	28
Glossary	30
Index	32

What Is a Rain Forest?

Imagine an early morning walk in a **moist** forest. Listen to the sounds of waterfalls and the songs of birds in the trees. A jaguar rests on a tree branch, watching a monkey swing from a **vine**. Other animals walk quietly on the leaf-covered forest floor. Above the trees, a layer of rain clouds keeps the air moist and warm. You are walking through a "rain forest." This name is used to describe a forest that is wet all the time.

When is a forest called a Rain Forest?

- Rain must fall very often, but not all day every day. There are only two seasons: the wet season and the dry season. Don't let the word "dry" fool you – in the dry season, it rains every day, but not as much as it does in the wet season!

- The temperature usually stays between 20°**C** and 34°C. The clouds protect the forest from too much sunlight, so it doesn't get extremely hot. The clouds keep temperatures about the same.

- All rain forests have certain types of plants, such as trees and bushes. There are also plants with long vines that need the support of trees to **survive**. Then there are ferns and **mosses,** and flowers such as orchids.

Rain Forests

The rainfall in rain forests ranges from 305 to 762 centimeters per year.

Layers of the Rain Forest

Tropical rain forests have four layers.
The plants and animals are different in each one.

The layers are often called:

- the forest floor
- the understory
- the lower canopy
- the upper canopy

There are different animals and plants at each layer. These animals have become used to their own levels of the forest. They have **adapted** to life at their levels. But to survive, they all need the special combination of *all* the levels. Many of the plants and animals that live in the rain forest are found nowhere else on earth.

The upper canopy

The lower canopy

The understory

The forest floor

The Forest Floor

The forest floor is at ground level. Only about 1% of the sunlight shining on the forest reaches this level. Mosses and **fungi** grow well here.

Busy leaf-cutter ants carry leaves to their ant nests. These ants are fungi farmers. After they collect the leaves in their nests, they add fungi to the pile. The fungi **break down** the leaves and make food for the ants.

Anteaters hunt for insects such as termites on the forest floor. The anteater has a sticky tongue that is 61 centimeters long. It's perfect for reaching into termite nests and getting the termites out.

Lizards, iguanas, snakes, spiders, insects, and other small animals also live on the forest floor.

The jaguar is the biggest meat eater in the forest. It climbs well and it runs fast. Its spotted coat is perfect **camouflage** for life in the rain forest.

This tapir is looking for something to eat.

An anteater

The Understory

The understory is the layer formed mostly by shrubs and trees which are less than 10 meters tall. These plants receive less light, rain, and wind than trees that reach the canopy.

The vine snake lives in the understory. Its camouflage makes it look like a harmless vine.

Red-eyed tree frogs, lizards, bats, moths, and butterflies are also found in the understory.

Some animals, such as monkeys and bush dogs, have very useful tails. They can use their tails to hold onto vines and branches, so they can climb easily in the trees.

Three-toed sloths and other kinds of **mammals** also live in the understory.

A sloth

A butterfly

A snake

A bush dog

Many birds build their nests in the understory. At this height, they are safe from animals that live on the forest floor.

The Lower Canopy

The forest's lower canopy is 32 to 46 meters above the ground. It collects and holds 80% of the rain that falls on the forest, so not much rain reaches the ground.

Plants called "epiphytes" hang from trees. These plants don't grow roots in the ground. Their roots hang in the air, where they take in the nutrients the plants need to survive.

Monkeys, bats, iguanas, and frogs also live in the lower canopy. Some of these animals never go down to the forest floor. There are plenty of insects, fruits, and birds for them to eat in the treetops.

Falling is always a danger, but different animals have different ways of staying safe. For example, tree frogs' feet have sticky pads that can hold them safely on slippery places.

A monkey's tail is like a fifth hand. It helps the monkey hold on to branches.

Toucans and other birds eat fruit and nuts. These birds help spread seeds through the forest because the seeds from the fruit and nuts they eat pass through their bodies and fall on the ground.

The Upper Canopy

The upper canopy is the highest layer of the rain forest. It is made of the tallest trees, which rise 23 to 76 meters above the ground. They are strong enough to survive the effects of wind, rain, and sunlight. The tops of the trees are shaped like open umbrellas, and the trees have pointed leaves, so the rain slides off easily. This keeps the trees from holding too much water, so they stay healthy.

These trees are very tall, but their root systems do not go deep into the ground. They spread out across the forest floor. Many of the animals and plants of the forest floor live among their roots.

Many kinds of insects live in the upper canopy, and they are often food for the birds there. There are also **reptiles** and **amphibians** living at this level.

Vultures, eagles, and other large birds build their nests in the upper canopy. These **predators** sit in the treetops and watch for **prey** down below.

One fifth of all the birds in the world live in the tall trees of the Amazon rain forest. One third of all birds live in rain forests some or all of the time.

People of the Rain Forest

People have lived in rain forests for more than 40,000 years. Living in small groups, they learned to find plants in the forest for food, and then to grow vegetables in small gardens. Their homes were made from the leaves and wood of forest plants. They also found how to use plants and animals of the forest to make medicine and **poison**. Hunters used the poison to kill animals for food. For many thousands of years, these people didn't have much effect on the **environment** because there weren't very many of them. They didn't use many of the **resources** found in the forest, either.

Today, about 1,000 different groups of native people live in rain forests. At one time, more than 6 million native people lived in the Amazon forest of South America. Today, there are only about 250,000. The forest is smaller now, and other people have moved in, bringing sicknesses that have killed the natives.

Some people still live deep in the rain forest and practice the old ways of life.

How the Ecosystem Works

The rain forest is a complete **ecosystem**, and every plant and animal that naturally lives there helps the system to succeed. For example, trees drop their leaves on the forest floor. Fungi and water on the forest floor break down the leaves. Then plants, birds, insects, reptiles, and other small animals can get food from the leaves. The animals also help the system when they pass waste from their bodies or become prey for larger animals.

Each thing that lives in the forest affects others. For example, if too many trees are cut down, there will not be enough leaves for the fungi to survive. Also, too much sunlight will come through the upper layers of the forest. Too much light hurts fungi and mosses on the forest floor. This will, in turn, hurt the insects and birds who need the fungi and mosses.

If birds and monkeys are caught and sold as pets, they cannot help spread seeds through the forest, so fewer trees will grow. In addition, if fewer birds and monkeys are hunting for food, the numbers of their prey will increase and create other problems.

Ecosystems in Danger

When people from outside the rain forests began to explore them, they created new problems for the forests. For example, they began to cut down trees to sell.

Rain forests are also hurt by farmers. In many areas, people have cut down bushes and vines and other plants and started fires to burn the trees down. After the fires, the farmers take out roots and rocks and use the land for farms. After one to five years, the soil is no good for farming any more, so the farmers move to a new area of the forest and start again.

When parts of forests are destroyed, the whole ecosystem is in danger. The animals who live in the forest must move, or they are killed by the fires. Animals lose their homes and the hunting areas they know, and then they have to go deeper into the forest.

Every year, people clear huge areas of forest for farms, roads, and **mines**. When the forest is smaller, fewer kinds of plants and animals can live there.

Trees, such as mahogany, are valuable for their hard wood, but they grow very slowly. It takes many years for new hardwood trees to grow in their place.

Destruction

The world's rain forests disappear at a rate of 80 acres per minute – day and night. People are destroying them by starting farms, cutting trees to sell, and creating **ranches**.

The **population** near rain forests has grown very fast, so farming families have to go deeper into the forest and clear more land. Then they can grow the food they need to survive. But the soil from the forest floor is poor. Sometimes, after only one year, the land is no good for planting. So the farmers move and clear a new area. They are destroying the rain forest, piece by piece.

Another reason for the destruction of large rain forest areas is the cutting of trees to sell. Trees can grow again in these areas, but it takes a very long time for the forest to return to normal.

The third big reason for rain forest destruction is ranching. People cut down large areas of trees to make places for their ranch animals.

Rain forests cover only 2% of the earth, but they have more than 50% of the different kinds of plants and animals in the world. When the forests are destroyed, different life forms are destroyed, too – forever. Every year, 50,000 kinds of plants and animals become **extinct**.

Trees from the rain forest are used to make newspapers, magazines, and building materials.

Scientists say that by the year 2020, 80–90% of the tropical rain forest ecosystems will be destroyed.

In the 1980s, almost 70,000 square kilometers of rain forest were destroyed to make cattle ranches.

Conservation

Tropical rain forests are the oldest and most valuable forests on earth. But today, these beautiful and important resources are in danger.

Governments around the world have begun to work together to find ways to stop the destruction of the rain forest. One problem is the fast-growing population. In 50 years, the population of the world will be about 10 billion people. Many of these people will live in poor countries, and most rain forests are in poor countries. We need to do something so that the people and the forests can both survive.

People around the world are learning more about the wonderful plants and animals that live in rain forests, and they are doing more to try to save them. Now, instead of paying people to cut down rain forest trees, some companies and governments are paying people to bring things out of the forest and still leave the forest healthy. If more and more companies and governments do this, we could save the rain forest from further destruction.

Some companies are working to keep rain forests healthy because they hope to find wonderful new lifesaving drugs or other products growing wild in the forest.

About one fourth of all the medicines that doctors use today come from rain forest plants.

Preservation: Butterflies

When people hurt the ecosystems of tropical rain forests by cutting down and burning forest areas, they hurt insects such as the Blue Morpha Butterfly. They can even make them extinct.

People are working in Central and South America to protect the Blue Morpha Butterfly from extinction. For example, they are building protected butterfly farms.

At these farms, the butterflies have places where they can safely lay eggs under leaves. After about ten days, small caterpillars come out of the tiny eggs. When they are grown, the caterpillars make their cocoons. They spend two weeks inside their cocoons, where they change into butterflies. When they come out, the butterflies continue the **cycle**.

Because of farms like these, thousands of butterflies are released into the rain forest. Butterfly farms help keep the Blue Morpha from extinction.

The butterfly above has just come out of its cocoon.

From the Author/Photographer

Fred Fusselman

I live in Colorado, U.S.A., and for the past 20 years, I have traveled around the world photographing and writing about interesting people and places. The locations I like best are far from cities or towns; places where unusual people and wildlife live.

I am a pilot, a sailor, and a diver, and I love outdoor activities. I am happy in or under the water, on the land, or in the air!

Tropical rain forests are rare, beautiful, and rapidly disappearing. Walking in a rain forest is a magical experience. Everything is alive!

From the Illustrator

Ralph Whirly

I live in Denver, Colorado, U.S.A., with my two children, Allison and Tommy, and my wife, Terri.

I enjoy illustrating books for children very much. I also have fun ballroom dancing.

Glossary

adapt – change over time to fit a situation or environment (page 6)

amphibian – an animal that can live on land and in water, such as a frog (page 14)

break down – go through chemical changes or separate into simpler parts; decompose (page 8)

C – [the abbreviation for] Celsius or Centigrade, a temperature scale on which the freezing point of water is 0° and the boiling point is 100° (page 4)

camouflage – coloring or other features that make an animal look like its environment so it is hard to see (page 9)

cycle – a series of related events that is repeated in the same order again and again (page 26)

ecosystem – all the animals and plants in an area and the way they relate to their environment and each other (page 18)

environment – the place where people, animals, or plants live and all the land, water, and air around them (page 16)

extinct – no longer alive; said of a plant or animal that doesn't exist anymore (page 22)

fungi – (plural of *fungus*) simple plants with no leaves that grow in dark, moist, warm places (page 8)

mammal – animals that feed their babies milk (page 10)

mine – a hole in the earth where people dig out things like gold, silver, and coal (page 21)

moist – a little wet; damp (page 4)

moss – a small green plant that looks like fur and grows on damp ground, trees, and rocks (page 4)

poison – something that causes sickness or death in anyone that eats, drinks, or breathes it (page 16)

population – the number of people living in an area (page 22)

predator – an animal that hunts and kills other animals for food (page 15)

prey – an animal that is hunted and eaten by another animal (page 15)

ranch – a large farm for raising herds of cattle, sheep, or horses (page 22)

reptile – a cold-blooded animal such as a snake, turtle, or crocodile (page 14)

resource – something such as land, water, or minerals in the ground that is valuable to the people in that country or area (page 16)

survive – continue to live even in difficult conditions (page 4)

tropical – related to the hottest and wettest parts of the world (page 6)

vine – a plant that grows long stems that attach to other plants or trees (page 4)

Index

birds 4, 11, 12–13, 14–15, 18
butterflies 10, 26–27
camouflage 9, 10
conservation 24
destruction 20, 22–23
ecosystem 18–19, 20, 23
farming 20–21, 22
floor 4, 6–7, 8–9, 18
fungi 8, 18
insects 8, 12, 14, 18
lower canopy 6–7, 12–13
mammals 10
medicine 16, 25
monkeys 10, 12–13, 18
people 16–17, 20–21, 22, 24–25, 26
plants 4, 6, 8, 10, 12–13, 14, 18, 24-25
preservation 26
rainfall 4–5, 10, 12, 14
reptiles 14, 18
temperature 4
understory 6–7, 10–11
upper canopy 6–7, 14–15